The Bird Orchestra

Dear Molly,

Thankyou for all your help and thoughtfulness during the lockdown. I was drawing these pictures as it was going on. Some of them may act as reminders! Ha!

much love
Charlotte x

The Bird Orchestra

Birdsong for a Pandemic

Rebecca Anderson-Deas and Charlotte Steel

Published in 2021 by Unlocked Press, an imprint of Dampier Press, Dampier House, Long Street, Sherborne, Dorset, DT9 3BY

unlocked@dampier.co.uk
www.charlottesteel.com

ISBN 978-1-8380710-3-5

Copyright © text Rebecca Anderson-Deas 2021
Copyright © illustrations Charlotte Steel 2021

The author and illustrator assert their moral right under the Copyright, Designs and Patents Act, 1988 to be identified respectively as author and illustrator of this work.

Designed by Wallis Agency www.wallisagency.co.uk

All rights reserved. No part of this book may be reproduced, stored in a retrieval system, or transmitted in any form or by any means (electronic, mechanical, photocopying, recording or otherwise) without the prior written permission of the publisher.

Unlocked Press is committed to a sustainable future for our books, our readers and our planet. This book is made from forest stewardship council certified paper.

Printed in the UK by Dampier Press

Foreword

When lockdown was announced I should have been practising and rehearsing for a concert that included Tchaikovsky's Fifth Symphony, which I had studied at school. It was featured on a film I watched the first weekend of lockdown and I was suddenly overwhelmed by sadness at not being able to play it because of the coronavirus pandemic.

Instead, I had found myself walking for miles on a fierce new daily exercise routine with the dogs, across fields, through woodlands, and, more troublingly, along the pavements of my home town, where I often had to quickstep into a distancing dance to avoid the increasingly numerous walkers and runners enjoying their own exercise ration. I found myself feeling oddly guilty about these walks and one afternoon, as I emerged from a woodland, I came upon two people armed with binoculars. I blurted out, like a guilty trespasser, that I had been listening to birds, at which the man asked if I had heard anything interesting, a blackcap or a goldcrest perhaps? Actually yes, I replied, and he then proceeded to discuss a number of more unusual birds that I was not at all sure I was able to identify as I was, and still am, only a novice. I did not know my birdsong as well as my Tchaikovsky, and felt rather intimidated by this man's obvious expertise. Pandemic walkers did seem to know their birds, unless this was a local wildlife expert I had heard mentioned by my husband? I asked him if he was called Nigel, expecting this stranger to think me more than a little odd. But this was indeed Nigel. Following the success of my bird expert identification, I decided to work on improving my birdsong identification skills. I wanted to be able to identify the birds by their song in the same way I could identify the different instruments of the orchestra by their sound.

I may not have access to my orchestra, but I did have wonderful local birds, my crutch since the traumatic death of my son, tragically young. I had found myself thinking and writing about them. A snatched radio programme went some way to explaining my new relationship with birds. One of the most common tattoos adopted by prisoners is the bird, a symbol of freedom, of course.

We were all prisoners now, of the coronavirus lockdown and I began to notice how many other people were also watching and listening to birds. A new venture was unlocked for me – my symphony orchestra of birds. I began assiduously working my way through a birdsong manual, and listening to birdsong recordings online. I thought I might have some fun positioning the most common British birds in my own bird symphony orchestra. We humans were no longer free to play, but the birds were in full voice.

It was tough 'auditioning' the birds, as they all seemed to be clamouring to join, even the ones I considered somewhat tonally challenged. I had to be brutal, turning away numerous crows, jackdaws and the odd raven, although I would certainly be inviting them to the concert, confident that such highly intelligent birds would make an appreciative audience.

I attempted to keep families of birds in the same section of the orchestra, an approach which was not always easy. Orchestral instruments also belong to different families, strings, woodwinds, brass and percussion. I was fearful that some human instrumentalists might not be happy with their bird representatives, so I prepared gentle reminders that this was lockdown and they should be grateful to any songbirds keeping their seats warm.

Lockdown soon began to feel like an eternity. My earliest feeling of liberation came when I heard my first skylark of the year, an obvious soloist for my concert. I began to envisage the concert as a double bill. I had already lined up the nightingale, but the skylark could be the violin soloist to the nightingale celebrity tenor.

I grew confident that my assembled Symphony Orchestra of Birds would do a worthy rendition of the Tchaikovsky, and I would be able to stomp, stride, stroll, meander, pause and listen, to a cheering and chirruping uplift of song, to accompany either an ascending lark or a meditative nightingale.

We were warned that the world would be changed when we emerged from lockdown. Experience told me that the world would be other, as it had been for me since losing my son. I do sometimes manage to soar with the lark, but my new normal is closer to the melancholy of Keats' nightingale. But, it remains a particular pleasure to listen to nightingales at night when other songbirds are silent. Their cadenza is a truly remarkable explosion of sunny sound into darkness.

It was not easy emerging into the cold light of day after our first lockdown, but at least we had the music of the birds. I hope you will enjoy this celebration of birds as you make sense of the post-pandemic world. In the words of Edward Thomas, the birds remind us that there are things 'not human yet of great honour and power in the world', that 'the earth is something more than a human estate.'

In this book we have featured memories and collective experiences of lockdown. Familiar collective nouns for birds have been complemented with some new suggested ones, as well as a slew of pandemic instrumental ones.

Keats' poem, a meditation on the unsatisfactory nature of pleasure and the inevitability of mortality, should perhaps remind us that all too often we humans take birds and other animals to reflect our own feelings. We should also perhaps be looking to their plight in this climate emergency we humans have created. We urgently need to protect the birds which serenade us, by taking better care of the bountiful planet we inhabit. This is how we will protect ourselves.

The Barn Owl
Tyto alba

Conductor

The conductor is the composer's messenger, interpreting, translating and delivering the music to the audience.

The conductor directs the orchestra to play the notes in the composer's score, setting the speed, shaping the phrasing and ensuring the different musicians play their music at the correct time. This is all done by gesture, with the help of a baton. Rehearsals take place beforehand, when there is an opportunity for preliminary verbal instruction.

Conductors can have many different names: director, master, maestro. They are alert to every note in the score.

Swooping elegantly and gracefully through the sky like a giant white moth, the barn owl is lovely to behold, but terrifying to hear. Its hissing screech – it is called a screech owl in the United States – somehow summons up the dark forces of night, which might explain its sinister reputation. It can be spotted in the late afternoon, a creature of the gloaming, the twilight zone between light and darkness.

Unable to roll their binocular eyes, wise owls instead rotate their whole heads, to watch the world around them. Our orchestra of songbirds may be fearful, as barn owls feed not only on small mammals, frogs and insects but also on birds. Musicians are often scared of the conductor, who is likely to notice any mistake they make.

During lockdown the pandemic parliament of owls told us to stay alert, and they made many rules, some rather frightening. Several orchestral players suspected they were brought in late, not when the music dictated.

Shopping List

- Violins
- Violas
- Cellos
- Double Basses
- Flutes
- Piccolos
- Oboes
- Clarinets
- Bassoons
- Saxophones
- Trumpets
- Trombones
- Horns
- Tuba
- Percussion

A stockpile of instruments

Just before we went into lockdown, there was panic buying in the shops as people began to stock up. Loo paper became an unobtainable luxury.

Strings

The smallest stringed instrument is the violin, and next biggest the viola. Both are held under the player's chin, resting on the left shoulder. The cello is much bigger, but not as big as the double bass. These two rest on the floor as they are too big to hold.

Stringed instruments are constructed out of pieces of wood glued together to form a hollow sound box. The quality of their sound is determined by the wood, and the varnish that coats it; the smaller the instrument the higher the sound, the better the wood, the richer the sound. Each instrument has four strings stretched across a bridge, attached to a tailpiece at one end and wrapped around an adjustable tuning peg at the other. Changing the length of the string changes the pitch (how high or low the note sounds). The player makes sound by plucking the strings, or, more often, by moving a bow across the string. The bow is made of wood and horsehair. Different notes are made by pressing fingers down on the strings to change the length of the part of the string that vibrates; the shorter the vibrating part, the higher the note.

The Wren
Troglodytidae

First violin

A chime of wrens

A briefing of first violins

Most numerous

The first violin often plays the tune in the orchestra, its brilliant sound carrying clearly over the other instruments. Orchestras have more violins than any other instrument.

Like the violin, the wren's song can soar above competing noise. For his small size, he is extraordinarily loud and explosive, (the French word for wren, le roitelet, means petty king!). He usually ends his short song with a dramatic and unmistakable trill and always sounds cheerful and positive. He does not fly off to warmer lands in winter and can be heard singing every day of the year.

Winter is a good time to listen out for wrens as very few other birds are singing.

They like to hide low in the hedge rather than high in the trees, feeding on insects and spiders, perhaps why they do not visit garden bird feeders. Although we may not see them as much as bird table visitors, they are the most common British bird.

The wren perfects his trill in the spring and keeps himself busy building several nests, so his partner has a choice. Wrens can choose very strange places to build their nests.

con fuoco

The Dunnock
Prunellidae

Second violin

The second violin supports the first violin's tune, not playing such high notes as the first. Second violins sometimes feel they do not have as much fun 'playing second fiddle'.

Dunnock means small, brown bird and he is a quieter creature, more of a background player than a show-off. He may not have the wren's dramatic trill and is not as loud, but his song is every bit as jaunty and cheerful. He often sings from the top of a bush, although, like the wren, he generally creeps around under the bushes like a mouse, feeding on insects, spiders and earthworms, and seeds and berries in winter. The dunnock starts singing at the first sign of warm weather, before most other birds. This is his opportunity to shine, as he is in full voice before most other birds find theirs.

Sometimes it is the quiet ones who have more fun. Male and female dunnocks have rather exciting personal lives. They are dating champions, with several girlfriends and boyfriends and complex families. Mrs Dunnock has multiple partners visiting her nest with food, and Mr Dunnock has several nests to visit. Dunnocks lay the most beautiful rich blue eggs.

Dating champion

con sordino

The Robin
Turdidae

Viola

The viola also plays a harmony to support the first violin's tune. It has a richer, warmer tone quality, sharing three strings with the violin but with a lower string instead of the violin's highest string.

The robin's song is rich and varied, soft and sometimes melancholic. It sounds stronger in spring and early summer, and softer and more wistful in winter. The robin may even be heard singing at night where there is street lighting.

One of the few birds to sing in mid-winter, he is often featured on Christmas cards, and is a national favourite. He only goes quiet in high summer when he is moulting and likes to keep a low profile. The female robin also sings!

appassionato

Humans love robins and they seem to love us, sometimes appearing almost tame. We like to imbue them with message and meaning.

A riot of robins

A protest of violas

Best loved

During lockdown there were many 'Black Lives Matter' protests.

The Great Tit
Paridae

Cello

An exercise of great tits

A workout of cellos

Most watched

> But why must I learn how to build a nest? I thought we liked using the bird boxes made by the humans.

The cello can do two jobs in the orchestra. Like our great tit, it can play a solid low accompaniment that is easily recognisable, but it can also astonish us with a beautiful soaring tune, taking us quite by surprise.

If you hear a loud two note call, it is likely to be the great tit. He announces winter's end and once he starts up he does not stop. He considers it his job to wake up all the other birds in the morning. He is the alarm call. His most recognisable song sounds like 'teacher teacher!' Listen for the emphasis on the first syllable.

The great tit actually has about forty different songs, so if you hear a bird and are not quite sure what it is, great tit might be a good guess. The way to recognise him is to identify his resonant and confident tone.

Along with blue tits, great tits are the most watched and studied British animals, and they love colonising our bird boxes. They feed on insects, mainly caterpillars and beetles, and berries and nuts in winter.

The demise of the sparrowhawk caused a population explosion of tits, so the recent return of these birds of prey has been a challenge for them. During the hawk-free years great tits became fatter, but now they are finding that they need to lose weight to escape this predator.

The Pheasant
Phasianidae

Double bass

The double bass is the largest and lowest stringed instrument and you need a large car to transport it, not a bicycle! The player has to sit on a high stool to play it. The double bass provides the orchestra's foundation. Without it the orchestra would not be grounded.

The pheasant is not native to the UK, and is only resident here because a few humans like to shoot it. The shooting season lasts from 1st October to 1st February and 40 million birds are released into the countryside every year for the sport.

The Victorians loved shooting, which was dangerous for our birds of prey as gamekeepers were so keen to protect their pheasants that they killed nearly all the red kites, buzzards, peregrine falcons and ravens. In recent years, these species have been reintroduced and protected.

Best at dying

An embarrassment of pheasants
A bicycle ride of double basses

Gamekeepers also used to clear woodlands of songbirds, destroying nests and shooting birds. One landowner set about killing all the nightingales as he thought their nighttime singing was keeping his pheasants from their beauty sleep!

The pheasant provides the foundation sound of the woods, crowing and clucking throughout the year. If you find yourself recording birdsong in woodland you will often hear pheasants in the background. They feed on seeds, grain, insects and earthworms.

Sometimes the exercisers were annoying – cyclists riding too fast and runners not distancing.

Woodwinds

The instruments in this family all used to be made of wood, but now they can be made of metal, plastic or a combination of materials. They are essentially tubes, with a mouthpiece at one end and an opening at the other, with rows of holes covered by metal caps called keys. Different notes are made by pressing on different keys. The sound changes depending on where the air leaves the instrument, through a keyhole or out of the open end. Air is blown into the instrument across the edge of, or into, the mouthpiece (flute, piccolo), between a single reed and a fixed surface (clarinet, saxophone), or between two reeds (oboe, bassoon).

The Blackcap
Sylviidae

Flute

The flute is a narrow metal tube which can either make a soft or a high, piercing sound. Like a violin, it can carry a tune high above the other instruments.

The blackcap is the king of the warblers, a bird family. Along with other warblers, it winters in northern Africa or southern Europe and journeys here in early spring. One of our most accomplished singers, he is also known as the mock nightingale, with his liquid, fluting song, sweet and loud.

Blackcaps sometimes stay here in winter if they don't fancy the long distance flight. They can be spotted at garden bird tables.

Best warbler songster

A confusion of warblers

The Goldcrest
Sylviidae

Piccolo

The piccolo is a tiny flute, which plays very high notes.

The goldcrest is Britain's smallest bird, singing from high up in the trees. His song is a high tinkle, a falsetto warble, like the sound of a dampened finger running across glass, so high pitched that its frequency cannot be heard by older humans. Goldcrests feed on tiny insects and spiders, and their eggs are like pale pinkish peas. They are resident here all year round.

Tiniest bird

A bake off of flutes and piccolos

dolce

The Whitethroat
Sylviidae

Oboe

Warbler rocker

A furlough of whitethroats

An idling of oboes

The oboe is made of wood and has a more mellow sound than the flute. It can also carry the tune with its bright, high range. It does not have a mouthpiece like the flute, but a double reed. When air is blown through the two reeds tied together, they vibrate to produce a rather melancholic sound.

The whitethroat makes a throaty sound, not as pure as the blackcap. He is the singer who sounds as if he smokes too much, or sings 'dirty'. The song is a fast and tuneless jumble of scratchy notes with a jerky rhythm, generally coming from the hedgerows and brambles. Sometimes whitethroats fly a few metres up into the air, and sing a longer, more varied song. They can look rather cross, glaring at you from the top of the hedge. This may be because they have reddish-brown eyes.

Whitethroats arrive from their sub-Saharan winter quarters mid-April to mid-May and depart August to September. They feed on insects, and berries in autumn.

cantabile

The Blackbird
Turdidae

Clarinet

A merle of blackbirds

Best known bird

A merlot of clarinets

The clarinet produces a warm, liquid sound when air is blown between a single reed and a mouthpiece. Sound is made by the vibrating reed. The clarinet can play nearly four octaves, a large range of low and high notes, which makes it extremely versatile. It is a popular choice at school.

Blackbirds are our most widespread and familiar garden birds, living here all year round. They are happy to live near humans, scouring our lawns and grassy areas for worms. They are not perhaps the most exciting looking birds and their name is uninspiring, but they have a beautiful and mellow song. The blackbird is our easy classics singer, recognisable to all, and always sounding ridiculously relaxed and positive.

In the nursery rhyme, the four and twenty blackbirds would have been placed in what the Tudors called a surprise pie, hidden under a pre-baked pastry crust just before being placed on the table. Dinner guests would be entertained watching them break out of the pie and fly off!

The expression 'to whistle like a blackbird' means to do something easily. Blackbird song sounds happy and lazy, boasting an easy life.

The Bittern
Ardeidae

Bassoon

The bassoon is a double-reeded instrument with a deep, bass sound made by blowing air between the reeds. The vibrating air travels over nine feet to the bottom of the instrument and then up to the top where the sound leaves the instrument.

The bittern is a shy bird. If you see one, it is likely to be in flight, looking like a cross between a giant tawny owl and a grey heron.

Bitterns live in large reed beds, carefully hidden from view, feeding on fish, amphibians and insects. Occasionally they feed on water voles or small birds. They are smaller, and more compact than herons, and boom a song like a foghorn, from January to April. The song resembles the sound made by blowing across the neck of a bottle. They boom day and night, the sound carrying up to five kilometres on a still night.

When hiding, bitterns flatten themselves with wings outstretched so they look like upturned umbrellas, with only their bills pointing up. They can stay very still, blending invisibly into the background.

Most shy

A sedge of bitterns

A protection of bassoons

misterioso

The Chiffchaff
Sylviidae

Saxophone

Simplest song

The saxophone is not a standard instrument of the symphony orchestra, more at home in a jazz band, and very popular in the school orchestra. It is something of a bridge from the woodwind to the brass section as it is made of brass, but uses a single-reed mouthpiece like the clarinet. It is more powerful than most woodwinds, and more versatile than most brass.

The chiffchaff's two-note tuneless ditty is the simplest of all birdsong. Like many other birds he is named after the sound he makes, forever singing, 'chiff chaff, chiff chaff'. He heralds the imminent arrival of spring. He is the promise of warmer weather, arriving in March, before the April rush of other migrant songbirds to our woods, meadows and gardens. He feeds on insects and spiders.

He is the last migrant bird to leave, if he leaves at all. Like the blackcap he sometimes prefers not to undertake the long distance flight to warmer southern climes.

tranquillo

There was increased stress during the pandemic, and some people tried to calm down with meditation.

A meditation of chiffchaffs
A chant of saxophones

Brass

Brass instruments are pipes that widen into a bell-like shape at the end, curved and twisted into shapes that make them easier to play and hold. Sound is produced when the players buzz their lips whilst blowing air through the mouthpiece, like 'blowing a raspberry'. Most brass instruments have valves attached to their long pipes, which open and close different parts of the pipe, thereby increasing the length of the pipe and the pitch of the note. In addition to managing the valves, the players can change their lip aperture and tension, known as embouchure, to create different pitches from a range of overtones or harmonics.

Trumpet

French Horn

Tuba

Trombone

The Goldfinch
Fringillidae

Trumpet

The trumpet is the highest brass instrument, with a clear, bright sound. This tube is over six feet long, bent into an oblong shape. It has been around thousands of years, often used to signal and send messages. The modern trumpet has three valves.

The brightness of the goldfinch song matches his dazzling, colourful plumage, but the sparkling and gleeful song does include a peculiar buzz. Too beautiful and tuneful for their own good, goldfinches were once captured and kept in cages, but they have made a remarkable comeback in recent years.

The industrial scale of goldfinch trapping in the nineteenth century almost caused their extinction by the start of the twentieth. Saving the goldfinch was one of the first tasks of the Society for the Protection of Birds, the precursor to today's RSPB.

Deeply symbolic, from health giving properties to fertility symbol, this is a bird featured in many Medieval and Renaissance paintings, famously in Hieronymus Bosch's Garden of Earthly Delights.

Goldfinches gather in great numbers in early autumn, feeding on seed-bearing weeds, a favourite being thistle.

The charm of goldfinches derives from the Old English word c'rim, meaning the blended tinkling sounds produced by a small flock.

Prettiest bird

A charm of goldfinches
A zoom of trumpets

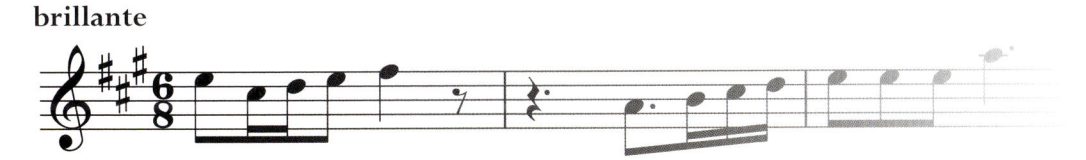

How many people had heard of Zoom before the pandemic? Now we were working, exercising and meeting friends and family on this social media platform.

Let's do a pub quiz next Friday.

We goldfinches are so lucky to have our own natural black and red face masks. We don't need disposable ones.

brillante

The Chaffinch
Fringillidae

Trombone

A gaming of chaffinches

A wicket of trombones

Best gamer

accelerando

The trombone is the mellow baritone of the brass family. Instead of valves and keys it uses a slide with seven positions to change the length of its nine foot tube and thereby the pitch of the note. It has an additional short tuning slide for adjusting intonation.

The chaffinch has been described as the fast bowler of songbirds. One of the first birds to sing in spring, in late February, he runs in, gathering speed, and builds up to a flourish, or 'cadence'. Three to four sharp notes segue into a series of lower pitched notes, culminating in a bright, rolling shiver. Chaffinch song lasts only a few seconds and is repeated over three thousand times in a day! The chaffinch is one of our most widespread songbirds, feeding on seeds, although the young are also fed insects. Resident here all year round, chaffinches are joined in winter by their migrant cousins from colder northern Europe.

They are named after their call. Whilst searching for seed in the chaff on the threshing floor, they seemed to say 'finch'. In reply to the yellowhammer's 'a little bit of bread and no cheese' the chaffinch will reply, 'I haven't had a bit of bread and cheese this five year'.

In addition to sport in the garden there was rather too much online gaming.

"My Victorian ancestors did competitive sport: singing contests in pubs. Humans bet money on which caged bird could sing the longest."

"Our lives are better. How horrible, living in a cage."

The Greenfinch
Fringillidae

Horn

This twenty foot tube is wound into a circle with a very large bell at the end, turned away from the audience. It produces a clear, mellow sound, often playing beautiful tunes. Different notes are produced by pressing valves with the left hand while the right hand moves inside the bell.

Greenfinch song somehow encapsulates all birdsong. Humans whistling like birds sound as if they are imitating the greenfinch, like the sound of a water-filled pipe imitating a bird, bubbling, liquid, unhurried and pretty. Listen out for his signature, a slightly rasping, descending glissando at the end of the phrase. Like the rallying sound of the battle horn, he can sing in flight, sending his trills out on the airwaves.

Greenfinches became our bird feeder champions, steadily climbing the RSPB garden league table. With a diet of shoots, buds, fruit and berries they are particularly partial to sunflower seeds.

Resident here all year round, they are joined in winter by their relations from colder countries.

I do like to sing on the wing.

Top piper

Have you got your mask?

A trembling of finches
A worry of horns

agitato

The pandemic generated so much fear and worry – distancing, masking up, hand washing, and mastering new technology. We went into battle against an invisible enemy.

Wash your hands before you wash your hands.

You must wash your hands for as long as it takes to sing Happy Birthday through twice.

The Bullfinch

Fringillidae

Tuba

The bass instrument of the brass family, this sixteen foot tube produces the lowest sounds. It is held upright in the player's lap and has four or five valves. It is the lonely instrument of the symphony orchestra as there is generally only a part for one tuba.

The bullfinch is a shy, reclusive bird, with an unhurried two note song, hardly a bellowing, more of a moaning. Both sexes sing a soft and slow mix of low, creaky notes.

Bullfinches have never been popular with farmers because of their fondness for eating early fruit tree flower buds. Their numbers were decimated by culling. They are sedentary birds, not keen on travel.

When they were caged in the nineteenth century it was thought that these compliant birds could be taught to sing for and by humans. To call someone a bullfinch was to call them a fool!

lacrimoso

A bellowing of bullfinches

A loneliness of tubas

Most reclusive finch

Hooray! Are you coming to bubble with me?

I am a little tired of counting so many rests! There is no one to talk to back here.

Too many people had to shield and isolate on their own, left to their books and puzzles.

Percussion

The percussion section has the largest number of different instruments. This family includes any instrument that makes a sound when the player hits, shakes or scrapes it, using the right amount of force, on the right part of the instrument, at just the right time. Some percussion instruments are tuned (they play particular notes), such as the xylophone, timpani (or kettle drums), bass drum and piano, while others are untuned, such as the snare drum, triangle, most cymbals and castanets.

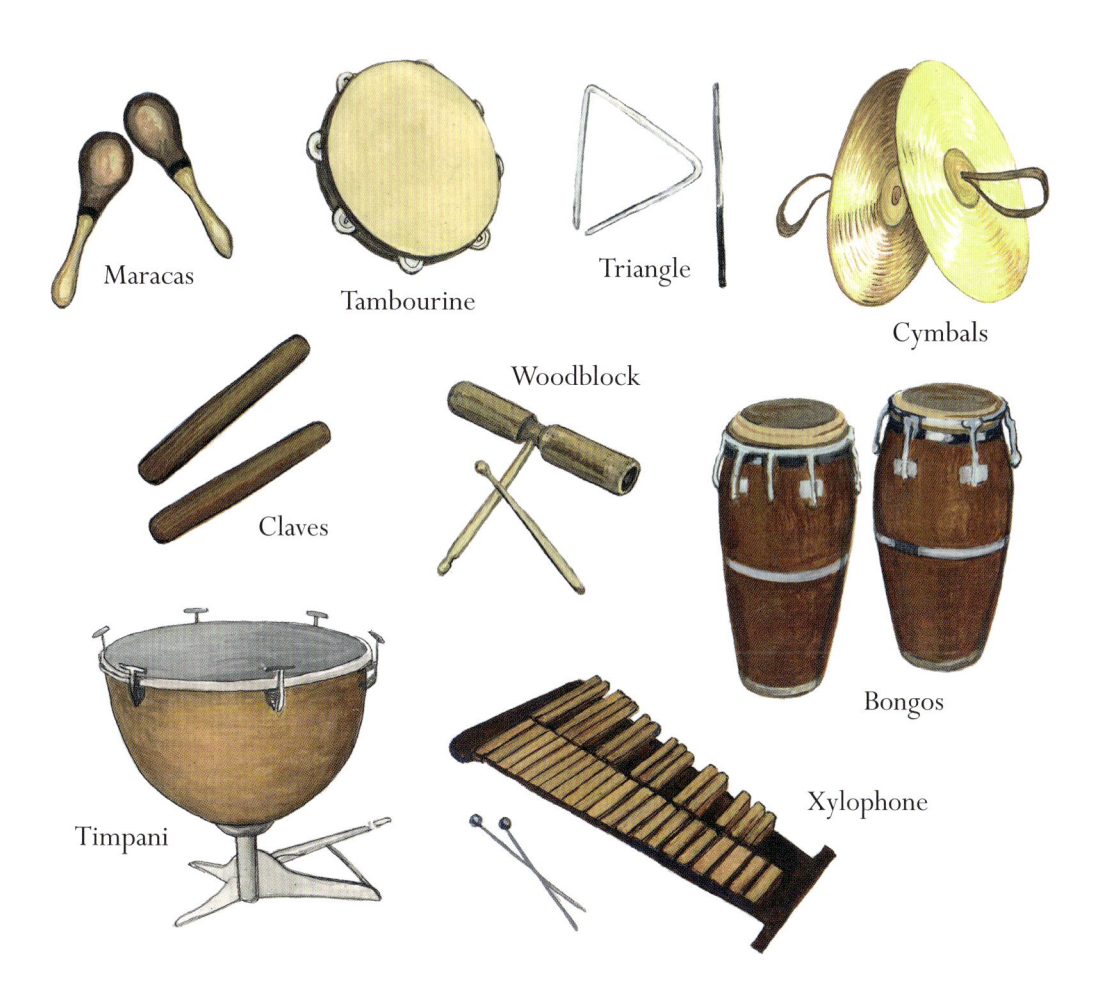

Maracas

Tambourine

Triangle

Cymbals

Woodblock

Claves

Bongos

Timpani

Xylophone

The Great Spotted Woodpecker
Picidae

Percussion

A descent of woodpeckers
A clap of percussion

The percussion section adds colour to the symphony orchestra: tone, rhythm and texture. The percussionist usually has to play several different instruments in one piece of music.

The Great Spotted Woodpecker is our most prolific woodpecker, and a greedy visitor to garden bird feeders. It does not need closed canopy woodland, but can thrive wherever there are trees. Both males and females drum on dry, dead or hollow wood to produce their magnificent rattle of percussive music.

The woodpecker's specially adapted skull has been studied by designers of motorcycle helmets. The muscles of the head and neck contract a split second before impact, acting as a shock absorber.

These woodpeckers can be seen spiralling around tree trunks, emitting a 'pik' call in joyous celebration of the drumming, and energetically swooping towards the tree before slapping into it.

Their diet consists mostly of insects, larvae and seeds but they also feed young tits and tits' eggs to their voracious young, who squawk continuously for food in the nest.

Greediest

During lockdown we applauded healthcare workers on a Thursday night, clapping and banging our kitchen utensils.

I love seeing that all my friends are alright on a Thursday night. It is fun.

Why aren't the neighbours at no. 7 out here clapping?

The Skylark
Alaudidae

Soloist

An exultation of skylarks

Top sprinter

Solo musicians are the film stars of the concert, the headliners. Their fame and reputation may be what sells tickets to the concert. They have to work with the orchestra, attending a few rehearsals before the concert. The sound of the soloist must be strong, rising above the orchestra.

The choice of music is important. The audience might be drawn to the concert by a favourite piece of music.

The skylark is famous for singing on the wing, as he rises higher and higher into the open sky, his concert platform. His continuous outpouring of quavering trills, whistles and chirrups can last for up to fifteen minutes without pause. George Meredith's poem, which inspired Vaughan Williams' The Lark Ascending (voted the nation's favourite classical piece of music), is a perfect evocation of the lark's flowing and fast-paced downpour of notes, the 'silver chain of sound'.

Skylarks nest on the ground, concealed in vegetation, and feed on insects, other invertebrates and seeds. They live here all year round, joined in winter by their relations from colder European climes.

Victorians liked to eat skylarks. At Leadenhall Market in London, at the height of their culinary popularity, up to 40,000 were sold in one day! But it is modern intensive farming which has decimated their numbers most.

volante

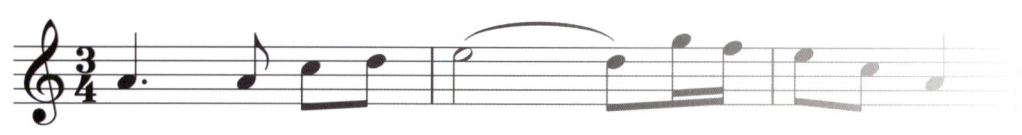

The pandemic assaulted the world of work and huge numbers of people were forced to work from home. Parents had to juggle working from home with home educating their children. While some people preferred it, others struggled to stay glued to their laptops.

I love working from home. I have never liked the commute to the office.

Are you there? I can neither see nor hear you — why are you not at your desk?!

HELLO?!!

Skylark
By John Clare

The rolls and harrows lie at rest beside
   The battered road; and spreading far and wide
     Above the russet clods, the corn is seen
    Sprouting its spiry points of tender green,
   Where squats the hare, to terrors wide awake,
Like some brown clod the harrows failed to break.
Opening their golden caskets to the sun,
  The buttercups make schoolboys eager run,
To see who shall be first to pluck the prize—
Up from their hurry, see, the skylark flies,
And o'er her half-formed nest, with happy wings
  Winnows the air, till in the cloud she sings,
    Then hangs a dust-spot in the sunny skies,
    And drops, and drops, till in her nest she lies
   Which they unheeded passed—not dreaming then
  That birds which flew so high would drop agen
  To nests upon the ground, which anything
May come at to destroy. Had they the wing
Like such a bird, themselves would be too proud,
And build on nothing but a passing cloud!
As free from danger as the heavens are free
  From pain and toil, there would they build and be,
   And sail about the world to scenes unheard
Of and unseen—Oh, were they but a bird!
So think they, while they listen to its song,
And smile and fancy and so pass along;
While its low nest, moist with the dews of morn,
Lies safely, with the leveret, in the corn.

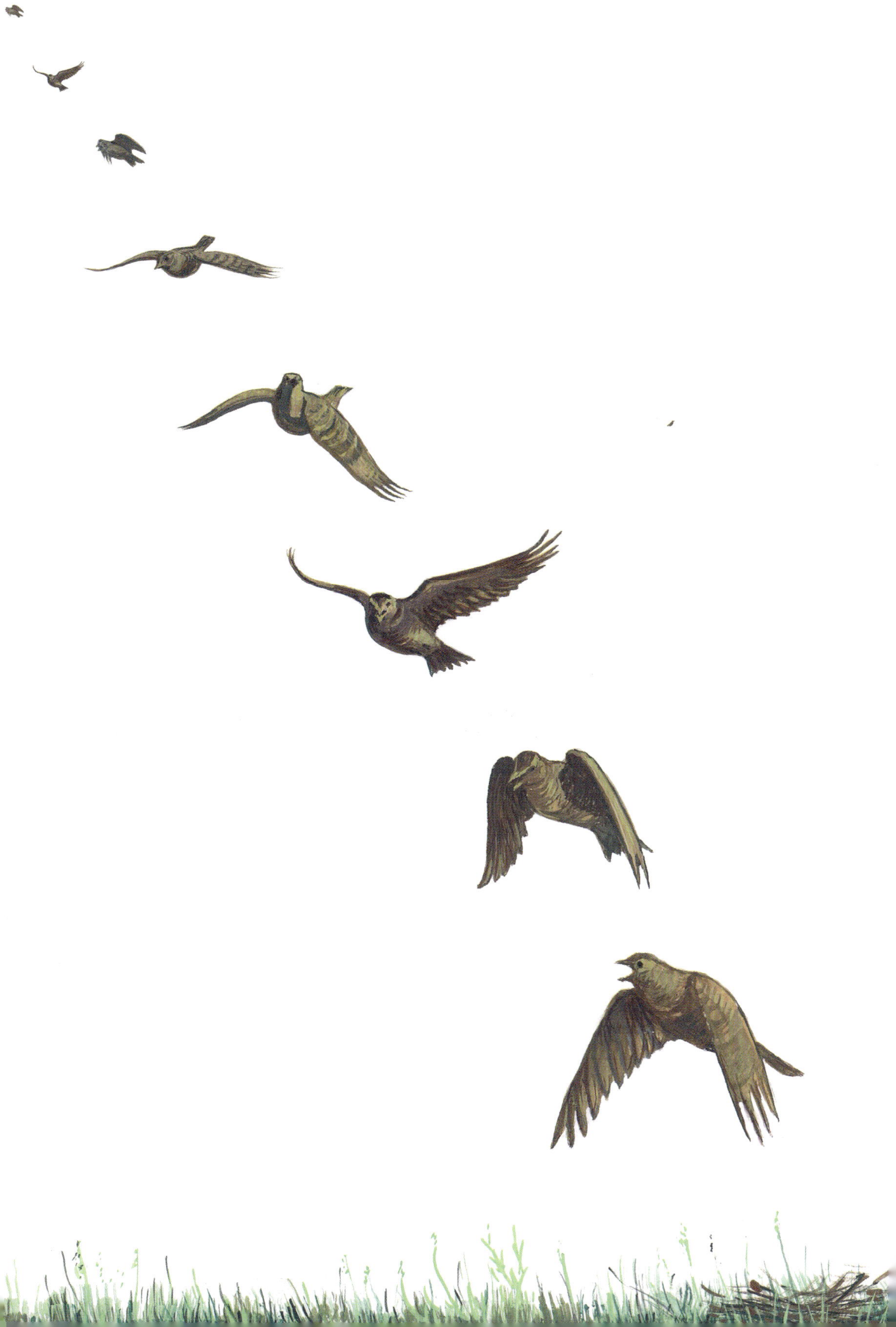

The Nightingale
Turdidae

Soloist

Singing champion

The nightingale is our celebrity tenor, the champion songster. He combines range and power, passion and volume. The slow, fluting piu piu which emerges from the darkness gathers in intensity and spills into a gurgling and rippling trilling, with added staccato firings and chucklings, all shaped into varied and rhythmic phrases. This bird has even perfected the dramatic use of silence between phrases, a pause for effect. A true bird artist, the nightingale is a master at blending sound and silence,

A watch of nightingales

melody and rhythm. In his repertoire there are 250 different phrases, composed of 600 different sounds.

Nightingales winter in central Africa, arriving here in April and leaving late July to September. Rarely seen, they need dense ground cover, coppiced woodland and hedge and scrub with brambles, to find their diet of insects. The male sings from mid-April to end May.

Southern England is something of a northern and western frontier for nightingales, which are more common in southern Europe. Their numbers have been so reduced that you need to visit areas they are known to return to. They will sing day and night, but unlike owls they sing not of night, but of the energy and joy of a sun-soaked afternoon!

Beatrice Harrison's famous 1924 recording, of a nightingale singing over her cello, was a BBC sensation, attracting over a million listeners.

Recent studies have noted that nightingales now have smaller wings, which means these long distance flyers will no longer be capable of flying as far.

affettuoso

tra - la - la - la,   tra - la - la - la - la - la.   Tra - la

The destruction caused by the pandemic will cause many people to lose their jobs, livelihoods and maybe their homes.

Forget your concert career, love. You might want to retrain as a computer programmer.

Which COVID test does he need to migrate south?

We won't be coming back here next year!

Ode to a Nightingale by John Keats

My heart aches, and a drowsy numbness pains
    My sense, as though of hemlock I had drunk,
Or emptied some dull opiate to the drains
    One minute past, and Lethe-wards had sunk:
'Tis not through envy of thy happy lot,
    But being too happy in thine happiness,—
        That thou, light-winged Dryad of the trees
            In some melodious plot
Of beechen green, and shadows numberless,
    Singest of summer in full-throated ease.

O, for a draught of vintage! that hath been
    Cool'd a long age in the deep-delved earth,
Tasting of Flora and the country green,
    Dance, and Provençal song, and sunburnt mirth!
O for a beaker full of the warm South,
    Full of the true, the blushful Hippocrene,
        With beaded bubbles winking at the brim,
            And purple-stained mouth;
That I might drink, and leave the world unseen,
    And with thee fade away into the forest dim:

Fade far away, dissolve, and quite forget
    What thou among the leaves hast never known,
The weariness, the fever, and the fret
    Here, where men sit and hear each other groan;
Where palsy shakes a few, sad, last gray hairs,
    Where youth grows pale, and spectre-thin, and dies;
        Where but to think is to be full of sorrow
            And leaden-eyed despairs,
Where Beauty cannot keep her lustrous eyes,
    Or new Love pine at them beyond to-morrow.

Away! away! for I will fly to thee,
    Not charioted by Bacchus and his pards,
But on the viewless wings of Poesy,
    Though the dull brain perplexes and retards:
Already with thee! tender is the night,
    And haply the Queen-Moon is on her throne,
        Cluster'd around by all her starry Fays;
            But here there is no light,
Save what from heaven is with the breezes blown
    Through verdurous glooms and winding mossy ways.

I cannot see what flowers are at my feet,
    Nor what soft incense hangs upon the boughs,
But, in embalmed darkness, guess each sweet
    Wherewith the seasonable month endows
The grass, the thicket, and the fruit-tree wild;
    White hawthorn, and the pastoral eglantine;
        Fast fading violets cover'd up in leaves;
            And mid-May's eldest child,
The coming musk-rose, full of dewy wine,
    The murmurous haunt of flies on summer eves.

        Darkling I listen; and, for many a time
            I have been half in love with easeful Death,
    Call'd him soft names in many a mused rhyme,
        To take into the air my quiet breath;
Now more than ever seems it rich to die,
        To cease upon the midnight with no pain,
            While thou art pouring forth thy soul abroad
                In such an ecstasy!
    Still wouldst thou sing, and I have ears in vain—
        To thy high requiem become a sod.

Thou wast not born for death, immortal Bird!
    No hungry generations tread thee down;
The voice I hear this passing night was heard
    In ancient days by emperor and clown:
Perhaps the self-same song that found a path
    Through the sad heart of Ruth, when, sick for home,
        She stood in tears amid the alien corn;
            The same that oft-times hath
Charm'd magic casements, opening on the foam
    Of perilous seas, in faery lands forlorn.

        Forlorn! the very word is like a bell
            To toll me back from thee to my sole self!
    Adieu! the fancy cannot cheat so well
        As she is fam'd to do, deceiving elf.
Adieu! adieu! thy plaintive anthem fades
    Past the near meadows, over the still stream,
        Up the hill-side; and now 'tis buried deep
            In the next valley-glades:
    Was it a vision, or a waking dream?
        Fled is that music:—Do I wake or sleep?

The Corvids

Corvidae

The Audience

An attention of spectators

Musicians can be nervous before performing to an audience, but it is important to remember that the audience is there to enjoy the performance, certainly not to terrify the players.

Corvids may not be songbirds, but they are highly intelligent, and it is fun listening to them punctuating the birdsong narrative: the carrion crow's 'caw, caw', the rook's more nasal, sonorous 'kraah', and the jackdaw's higher pitched, staccato 'jack, jack'. These three black corvids can be seen flying together, and will happily sit alongside each other in our audience.

The beautifully coloured jay, our British 'bird of paradise' is smaller and rather shy. He may want to sit at the back. You might not like his harsh, grating shriek but he is a skilled mimic. He can imitate other corvids, tawny owls, and, on occasion, dogs and cats. He feasts on acorns, performing the additional job of planting oak trees when he squirrels acorns underground. More of a woodland dweller, he is not as adapted to human areas as other corvids. The black and white magpie has a laughing chatter, and a somewhat undeserved reputation for raiding songbird nests, as he feeds mostly on insects, fruit and seeds. He is not quite the thief of superstition.

Larger than a buzzard (if you exclude the wing span), the raven is our requiem bird of myth and legend, and not as widespread as other corvids. He has a deeper craw sound. Highly intelligent, ravens have been spotted sledging in the snow, for the fun of it.

A murder of crows

My review in the Corvid Chronicle will be a killer.

A mischief of magpies

That magpie has stolen my seat.

Most unloved

A kindness of corvids

A parliament of rooks

A conspiracy of ravens

"This free school meal is a disgrace, you rip-off raven!"

"I enjoy being an essential worker."

A train of jackdaws

A scold of jays

Kind neighbours delivered food and medicines to vulnerable people.

The Performance is a Twitter Storm

Our songbirds may be singing for their lives, and for ours.

The Corvid Critics

Coming out of lockdown was always going to be harder than going into it. It was impossible knowing how to govern and how to behave. Holidays, quarantine, eat out to help out, rules of six, more lockdowns; the only trusted exit was a vaccine.

I love eat out to help out! — jackdaw

Don't you mean eat out to help the spread? — raven

It's not helping your spread. — rook / chough

jay

A misery of lockdowns

A terror of variants

Not another lockdown! — magpie

I do wish they would stop saying Corvid 19 when they mean COVID 19! — hooded crow

I was fined for having an illegal party. — carrion crow

62

Acknowledgments

Charlotte and Rebecca met at Fox Primary School in West London in the 1970s and have been friends ever since. Their memories of school are not of hard work, assessments or testing, but of a dazzling array of creative activities in which they happily participated. They would like to acknowledge all their Fox class teachers, as well as Mr Ivor Cutler, whose exceptional weekly lessons gave them poetry, jazz, drumming and dancing, in the same George Hall where Rebecca had her first ever violin lessons with Miss Harrison.

Charlotte would like to remember her grandmother, who showed her that even the tiniest creatures are precious, and who painted exquisite birds herself. Rebecca would like to thank her children, Rachel and Jamie, for encouraging her to turn a new obsession with birdsong into a picture book, her friends for their contributions of anecdotes, feathers, online links, articles, photographs, and proofreading, and her husband Bill, for his printing and woodland expertise, which made the production of this book possible, and provided woodland settings for much of the bird listening. She must, of course, acknowledge her dogs, Ruby and Doris, for enticing her on all those long walks through the woods.

For readers wanting to take their bird watching and listening further, we recommend Simon Barnes' transformational *Bird Watching with your Eyes Closed* and Mark Cocker and Richard Mabey's outstanding *Birds Britannica*. Sound recordings and video footage of all the songbirds featured in *The Bird Orchestra* are easy to find on the internet.

We would like to thank Nick Morris for giving us beautiful book design with musical accompaniment.